DOR
COMM
AND GREENS

BY RODNEY LEGG

THE
OPEN SPACES
SOCIETY

25A Bell Street, Henley-on-Thames, Oxon RG9 2BA
Telephone: 01–491–573–535

Supported by the

COUNTRYSIDE

Publishing details. First published 1995, by the Open Spaces Society [formerly and formally known as the Commons, Open Spaces and Footpaths Preservation Society], from its offices at 25a Bell Street, Henley-on-Thames, Oxfordshire RG9 2BA. 01–491–573–353.

Compiled and illustrated by Rodney Legg, with text, captions, and photographs being © Rodney Legg 1995.

Updatings may be sent to the author via the book's designers: Dorset Publishing Company, Wincanton Press, National School, North Street, Wincanton, Somerset BA9 9AT. 01–963–32583.

Printing credits. Typeset and printed by F.W.B. Printing at Bennetts Mead, Southgate Road, Wincanton, Somerset BA9 9EB. 01–963–33755.

Distribution. Locally, in Dorset, by Maurice Hann, from 36 Langdon Road, Parkstone, Poole, Dorset BH14 9EH. 01–202–738–248.

International standard book number [ISBN] 0 946574 08 1.

Contents

Introduction

This, hopefully, will be the first of many books. Not by me, though I would welcome the challenge to venture beyond my beloved county, but as a model for similar descriptions and celebrations of the common land heritage of England and Wales. Dorset comes quite low in the league table, given that the two countries have a total of 1.3 million acres of registered common land, which is the largest reserve of uncommitted semi-natural landscape this side of Hadrian's Wall.

Scotland excludes itself, due to different laws and practices, so there are no comparable relics of ancient land tenure north of the border. That said, common grazing and other shared rights was a custom taken by colonial settlers to distant past and present possessions of the British Empire, from Boston, Massachusetts, to Stanley Common in East Falkland.

Here in Dorset we have a traditional English shire-county mix of registered commons and greens. They include remnants of once extensive downland sheep-leazes, and heathland peat-turf and gorse-gathering wilderness. Plus droveways and ponds between the hills and market towns, with pounds for the arrest of stray animals.

Best at defending their mediaeval and pre-conquest rights were the people of Portland who registered claims to do and remove just about anything possible and impossible — many existing in theory rather than fact — along the southern length of the Chesil Beach and across the almost equally inhospitable stone plateau. Portland is like another country; they do things differently (or as they always have done) in the Isle and Royal Manor, and refer to mainlands as "kimberlins".

Most of these possibilities are not public in the general sense, being reserved as a privilege for certain residents, though in the case of former urban and borough commons, as determined by their pre-1974 boundaries, the right has been extended to the rest of us in the form of a statutory freedom to roam.

Similar opportunities are enjoyed over National Trust commons. Rights of access, to local people for "lawful sports and pastimes" extend to village and town greens. Where there is no legal right of access is to rural commons generally, though many that are still open and unenclosed so do have de facto public access by custom and tradition.

It is the longstanding and continuing aim of the Open Spaces Society — which was founded as the Commons Preservation Society in 1865 — that Parliament should extend public rights of access on foot "for air and exercise" to all registered common land. This was urged and envisaged, with a framework for bye-laws and management, by the multi-interest Common Land Forum.

Meanwhile in the deeper countryside we largely rely for our access on the proximity of public roads and the network of bridleways and footpaths which touch or cross many of the commons. Where these are mentioned in the text their parish numbers are given, being from the county maps of definitive rights of way that are compiled by Dorset County Council.

Knowing the name of the parish is the key to using those maps and this guidebook. Each common and green is listed under the parish or borough in which it lies. There is an Ordnance Survey map reference at the start and the official registration number (or numbers in the case of adjoining multiple registrations) is at the end of the listing. "CL" stands for common land and "VG" for village (or town) green.

Acreages are given at the beginning of the descriptions and public access opportunities, or the lack of them, are highlighted. General descriptions are intended to give a pen picture of the landscape with additional potted notes on significant aspects of the history, vegetation and wildlife.

Emphasis is given to ancient monuments because they are usually well preserved on commons, in scenic settings that display a visual continuity of land use back through the Middle Ages to the depths of antiquity. It is added value that the common itself represents a living piece of archaeology.

For this reason the Open Spaces Society campaigns to preserve their character by keeping them open and unenclosed. It also fights to protect them from encroachments and threat of deregistration. Through the society I was able to block an attempt at removing Poundbury Camp, above Dorchester, from the commons register. We have also persuaded the National Trust that it should have a long-term aim of returning King Down holding, at Pamphill, to sheep-grazing downland.

If you enjoy these Cinderella areas of time-warp landscape from a lost age, then the way to cherish them is with a donation and membership application to the Open Spaces Society. Many will need active intervention if they are to survive into their second millennium.

This book has come about because of national and local support. As well as the endorsement of the Countryside Commission, I am delighted to acknowledge help received from Sir John Smith and the Manifold Trust; from Dorset County Council; Purbeck District Council; Weymouth and Portland Borough Council; and Richard Harland. I am also grateful to my typesetter, Julie Green, and to Kate Ashbrook, Paul Johnson, and John Pitfield for scanning the proofs.

My hope is that this guidebook is worthy of the confidence that they have all shown, and for it to inspire similar coverage in other counties.

R.L.

AFFPUDDLE   SY 820 912
Throop Heath
2.5 acres, being a strip of unafforested land beside the unfenced lane from
Moreton Drive junction to the next junction half a mile north. Listed as
belonging to Turners Puddle parish but Throop and its former heath are in
Affpuddle.

It seems to be on the Affpuddle side of the boundary, and to have been
left as a firebreak, which part still is.

Affpuddle bridleway number 26 strikes off across it from the northern
extremity and becomes Turners Puddle bridleway 12 for the rest of its course
to Lawrence of Arabia's Cottage at Clouds Hill.

Registered unit CL 284.

AFFPUDDLE   SY 799 911
Waddock Cross
1.52 acres, in a triangle of dense woodland opposite the buildings at this
crossroads on the B3390. There are tarred public roads on each side.

Registered unit CL 355.

ALDERHOLT   SU 094 126
Bridleway Green
1.5 acres of what is claimed to have been an old roadside green, beside
bridleway number 26. It has hedges with a variety of woody species,
indicating antiquity.

Alderholt was the most vigilant parish in the county during the
commons registration process [1967-70], with results that contrast with
villages unmentioned here because they failed to protect any land.

Registered unit VG 34.

ALDERHOLT   SU 091 122
Cripplestyle Chapel
0.2 acres, adjoining the sad memorial garden to the demolished Ebenezer Old
Chapel. This was cob-walled and thatched, home-made by its own
worshippers [1807]. The roof and walls decayed and it collapsed [October
1976]; long after replacement by the nearby Williams Memorial Chapel [1888].

Registered unit CL 161.

ALDERHOLT   SU 118 136
Grass Triangle (1)
0.03 acres, being a tiny area of grass between Alderholt and Sandleheath, to
the south-west of Home Farm.

Owned by the parish council.

Registered unit VG 33.'

ALDERHOLT   SU 128 133

Grass Triangle (2)

0.05 acres, on the south side of the road into Fordingbridge, bounded on its southern boundary by footpath number 6, on Bonfire Hill.

Registered unit CL 160.

ALDERHOLT   SU 120 137

Home Farm Pond

0.17 acres, mainly grass, at the junction of footpath number 1 and the road to Alderholt Bridge in the north-east corner of Dorset.

Registered unit CL 163.

ALDERHOLT   SU 095 123

King Barrow Hill

23.62 acres, covered by two registrations and including the gorse-covered slopes and summit of King Barrow. This is ascended by footpath number 18 and was the setting for an annual pilgrimage from the nearby Cripplestyle Chapel on the Thursday of Whit Week. William Bailey first led his flock up the hill and hoisted a flag with the words "Feed my Lambs" [1807].

Footpaths 40, 18 and 39 converge. The "barrow" appears to be a natural conical knoll, rather than a burial mound. Dartford warblers breed here.

Registered units CL 253 and CL 162.

ALDERHOLT   SU 104 126

War Memorial

0.05 acres, on which the villagers erected a granite cross to remember their 18 men who fell in the Great War [1914-18]. It cost the village £120 [1920]. The ground is owned by the parish council.

Registered unit CL 159.

ASHMORE   ST 913 178

The Pond

0.1 acres, being the reason for Ashmore's location and existence. The village, at 705-feet on the top of Cranborne Chase, was *Ash-mere* in Old English, named for the trees around its pond. This was already ancient, being twice as old as Christianity in these parts, dating back to 1,000 BC in the Late Bronze Age. Ashmore is unique in being a village clustered around the archetypal prehistoric dewpond, man-made with a puddled clay base.

Despite the term it relies on rainfall rather than condensation. Evaporation was kept to a minimum by a coldness achieved by a combination of altitude and great depth. That was 16-feet. Traditionally a feast would be held on the rare occasions when it dried out, and the accumulated silt was then removed, in hundreds of cart-loads of fertile ooze which was then spread on the land.

The pond is circular and some 120 feet in diameter. It lies at the centre of the village, beside the junction of its three streets, and is overlooked by photogenic thatch. Ownership is vested in the parish council.

Registered unit VG 65.

ASHMORE   ST 922 162
Triangular Common
0.3 acres beside the junction of bridleways 7 and 23, on 525-feet downland south of Well Bottom. One of the "gore commons" of Cranborne Chase — the word being used for the triangular remnant of open field that was created when a pattern of rectangular furlongs had been drawn up.

Registered unit CL 151.

BEAMINSTER   ST 497 095
Beaminster Down
129.55 acres, almost entirely fenced and ploughed under wartime agricultural regulations [1940]. Despite the arable crops it enjoys the best public access of any non-urban common land in Dorset — a network of intersecting paths, being bridleways 17, 16, 10, 18, 6, 8, 7, 9 and 15, plus footpath 12 beside Down Farm. Two Bronze Age round barrows are scheduled ancient monuments.

Registered unit CL 40.

BERE REGIS   SY 848 947
Court Pound
0.25 acres, east of the parish church, beside the Wool road to the south of the Royal Oak. Probably established as a timber stockade at a price of £1 0s 4d recorded in churchwardens' accounts [1608]. The present south wall is in stone removed from the ruins of the Manor House in the nineteenth-century.

Registered unit CL 67.

BERE REGIS   SY 844 948
Soulsmoor, also known as **The Marsh** or **The Moor**
6.97 acres of spongy meadow between the village and the Bere Stream. Visible from footpath number 30 which runs close to its southern side, from the hamlet of Shitterton (as on its road sign) or Sitterton (as on the map) to Southbrook.

Registered unit CL 66.

BINCOMBE

SY 671 860

Ridgeway Hill

0.42 acres of scrubby roadside waste, in the triangle formed by the modern A354 and the old lane that runs almost parallel to it, a little to the west, directly over the hill and down into Upwey. Bounded to the south by bridleway number 14.

Registered unit CL 344.

BLOXWORTH

SY 878 940

Bloxworth Green

16 acres, south and south-east of the village, extending through the woods beside unfenced sections of the lane and the A35, plus footpath number 7 and strips of land in Humber's Coppice and the west of The Knoll.

Registered unit VG 53.

BLOXWORTH

SY 882 946

The Green

3.4 acres of grass and trees around the bus shelter at the junction in the centre of the village. Merges into the surrounding woods.

Registered unit CL 8.

BOTHENHAMPTON

SY 487 923

Poor Lots Common

0.47 acres of hilltop above the strip lynchets of the steep slope rising from Bonscombe, with footpath number 23 passing beside it. This crosses the hill from the west end of Walditch to join footpath 23, which continues to Burbitt Lane, Shipton Gorge.

Registered unit CL 33.

BOTHENHAMPTON

SY 483 926

Walditch Village Green

0.4 acres of grass with a chestnut tree and an ornamental border, beside the road in the centre of the village.

Given to the parish council by C.J.G. White [1970].

Registered unit VG 69.

BOURNEMOUTH

SZ 128 953

Holdenhurst Village Green

0.2 acres, of neat grass around which cottages are clustered at the heart of the former mother parish of Bournemouth, complete with a Saxon church until this was replaced by the Victorians [1839]. Wooden posts protect it from stray cars in a time-warp cul-de-sac beside the River Stour meadows.

Owned by the Borough of Bournemouth.

Registered unit VG 1.

BOURNEMOUTH   SZ 070 965
Kinson Green
0.2 acres of grass next to the library and bus-stop, beside Wimborne Road at
the heart of this busy suburb. Created when the village school was
demolished. Owned by the borough council and crossed by footpath E52.
Registered unit VG 2.

BOURNEMOUTH   SZ 156 920
Wick Village Green
0.2 acres, formerly used for the winter storage of furze-faggots from gorse
gathered by the cottagers of Wick and Tuckton for their bread-ovens. Became
the site of an annual village festival, called Dossum Festweek, with traders'
stalls and evening dancing. Thomas Hardy is reputed to have first seen the
ring dance here. Finally held during the last August of peace before the Great
War [1913].
Now suburban mown grass with three cherry trees. Owned by the
Borough of Bournemouth.
Registered unit VG 3.

BRADFORD PEVERELL   SY 650 935
Riverside Meadow
0.4 acres, being part of a field next to the River Frome. No public access.
Registered unit CL 302.

BRADFORD PEVERELL   SY 680 914
West Ward Meadows
3.55 acres in an isolated ox-bow of the River Frome bounded by the water to
the north and the railway to the south. As with similar water-meadows, rights
of grazing for horses and cattle were restricted to the period 15 August to 1
November, in order to keep the land clear for winter inundation and summer
cuts of hay.
Owned by the Prince of Wales, in his capacity as Duke of Cornwall. No
public access.
Registered unit CL 322.

BUCKLAND NEWTON   ST 693 054
Recreational Allotment
4.4 acres of grass, otherwise known as "Four Acre" or "The Rec", with a mown
sports area and the remainder cut for silage. West of the road at Woolford's
Water, with footpath number 9 along its north side.
Owned by the parish council.
Registered unit VG 27.

BUCKLAND NEWTON　　　　　　　　　　　　　　　　ST 686 052
Village Pound
0.1 acres, being a square of grass beneath a tree on the western side of the village, near the road junctions of bridleway number 46 and footpath 48.
　　　Owned by the parish council.
　　　Registered unit VG 62.

BURSTOCK　　　　　　　　　　　　　　　　　　　　ST 435 024
Burstock Common
7.6 acre strip of valley side, ranging from lanky grass to dense woodland, southwards from the hamlet to the B3164 and then around the cottage gardens and either side of footpath number 5.
　　　Registered unit CL 68.

BURTON　　　　　　　　　　　　　　　　　　　　　SZ 167 948
Burton Green
0.7 acres, roughly triangular, of grass, oaks and ornamental trees, between Salisbury Road and Footners Lane. Burton Grange, the United Reformed Church, shops and cottages face on to it.
　　　Registered unit VG 146.

CASTLETON　　　　　　　　　　　　　　　　　　　ST 616 148
Charlock Hill
0.1 acres beside the B3148 north of Sherborne, beneath a clump of trees where the public roads Checcombe Lane and Coombe Road form a crossroads with the main road.
　　　Registered unit CL 345.

CHALDON HERRING　　　　　　　　　　　　　　　SY 791 383
The Green
0.2 acres in a grassy triangle, set amid the cottages in East Chaldon. Literary associations with Sylvia Townsend Warner [1893-1978] and Valentine Ackland [1906-69] living in Miss Green's cottage on the Sailor's Return side of the green [1930-33]. Novelist Theodore Francis Powys [1875-1953] lived at Lilac Cottage and set his classic *Mr Weston's Good Wine* [1925] in and around the village. By this time he had moved to Beth Car, a house beside the lane towards West Chaldon.
　　　The green is owned by the parish council.
　　　Registered unit VG 7.

CHARMINSTER   SY 678 297
The Square
0.05 acres of car-parking, plus a commemorative oak planted for the centenary
of Dorset County Council [1989]. There are buildings on three sides and Birds
Lane on the other.. Owned by the parish council, who have also taken
possession of the site of the former forge [demolished 1970].
    Registered unit VG 61.

CHARMINSTER   SY 674 922
West Ward Common
38.75 acres, adjoining similar water-meadows on the Dorchester side of the
parish boundary. Traditionally inundated in winter, to protect the land from
frost, and consequently grew lush early hay. Secondary cuts followed.
    This caused the turning out of stock to be strictly limited, with cow
grazing between 6 to 14 August and then heifers and horses from 15 August to
1 November. Crossed by footpath number 14 in the south-east corner, near the
A37 roundabout. No other public rights of way.
    Registered units CL 35, CL 52 and CL 147.

CHESELBOURNE   ST 760 001
Village Green
0.1 acres of grass beside the stream at the road junctions in the centre of this
attractive chalkland village.
    Owned by the parish council.
    Registered unit VG 23.

CHICKERELL   SY 651 798
Puxey Pond
0.27 acres of former brickyard claypits on the west side of Puxey Lane. Owned
by the parish council.
    Registered unit CL 116.

CHILD OKEFORD   ST 822 130
Netmead or **Nutmead**
43 acres of riverside pasture in the Blackmore Vale. The rushy River Stour
meanders for half a mile along the western side of these buttercup meadows.
    Crossed by two public paths. Child Okeford footpath number 10 strikes
off south-east from Netmead Lane which is an untarred public road westward
from the northern end of the village.
    The other access is via footpath number 24, heading west from the east
end of Greenway Lane, a short distance from the centre of the village.
    On the east side of the former millpond on the southern stretch of river
is a footbridge which takes the path to Bere Marsh Farm and Shillingstone.
Kingfishers are almost commonplace along these tranquil reaches.

Spitfire N3231 of 609 Squadron from RAF Warmwell would have disturbed their ancestors, by plunging from 21,000 feet during a Battle of Britain dog-fight [7 October 1940]. Pilot Officer Michael Staples had baled out.

Registered unit CL 347.

CHRISTCHURCH   SZ 213 943
Chewton Common
83.14 acres of scrub, trees and rough grass which survived challenges to its common land status in the High Court [1977]. This held that as long as waste land of a manor could be shown to have been owned by the lord of the manor at some stage in the past, it did not have to be owned by the lord of the manor at its date of registration, in order for the claim to be valid.

What has been saved is otherwise prime urban building land that is the principal green lung for northern Highcliffe. Footpath 29 runs its entire length, south to north, and paths 30 and 31 branch off eastwards. There is also a general right of public access "for air and exercise" under section 193 of the Law of Property Act 1925.

Registered units CL 190 and CL 269.

CHRISTCHURCH   SZ 173 922
Fisherman's Bank
1.72 acres, of what is in effect Stanpit creek, on Christchurch Harbour, with a narrow strip of gravel and grass between the shore and the houses. It faces the reed beds of Stanpit Marsh. Footpath number 22 runs its length, a third of a mile, and there is a general right of public access "for air and exercise" under section 193 of the Law and Property Act 1925.

These days there are few fishermen or nets but there is still much boating bustle and even more unattended craft pulled up along the shore. Usually both interesting and picturesque.

Registered unit CL 243.

CHRISTCHURCH   SZ 160 930
Millhams
40.54 acres of riverside pasture on the west bank of the River Avon, either side of the A35 as it enters the town. No public paths have been claimed across it but there is a general right of access "for air and exercise" under section 193 of the Law of Property Act 1925.

Registered units CL 160 and CL 19.

CHRISTCHURCH   SZ 155 928
Recreation Ground
8.9 acres, allotted to the town "as a place of exercise and recreation" by an enclosure award [1876]. Also doubles as a municipal park with an avenue of

limes, raised flower beds, and a garden commemorating the town's links with Christchurch, New Zealand. South-west of the big roundabout at the north end of the High Street.
Registered unit VG 90.

CHRISTCHURCH and HURN   SZ 145 953
Town Common, Coward's Marsh and Ogber
358.47 acres of wooded gravel plateau, heathland slopes, and the western meadows of the River Avon. It is a glorious landscape package, dominated by St Catherine's Hill, with views over Christchurch Priory and Harbour, and eastwards into the New Forest.

The mediaeval St Catherine's Chapel, named for the patron saint of spinsters, has left only indistinct traces but there are a number of Bronze Age round barrows. Crossed from north to south by the dismantled trackbed of a branch railway from Ringwood to Christchurch [1845-1945], which can be followed for three miles.

More intrusively, the northern sector is punctured by the A338 dual carriageway. Roads that have access are further south, from the hillside estates at Fairmile, and the main upland common is crossed or reached by bridleways 3, 4 and 7, and by footpaths 58, 46, 55 and 11.

Coward's Marsh and Ogber are a distinct offshoot, both visually and physically, extending north-east beside the River Avon. Here there are no official paths but a general access right still applies, "for air and exercise" under section 193 of the Law of Property Act 1925.
Registered units CL 18, CL 158 and CL 159.

CHURCH KNOWLE   SY 941 816
Boshards Green
0.82 acres, beside footpath number 20, south of Church Farm. Appears as "Beshard Green" on the parish tithe map [1842] and should probably have been claimed as a green rather than common land.
Registered unit CL 13.

COLEHILL   SU 023 013
Deans Bush
4 acres, north-east of St Michael's Church, this triangle of wild land being a virtual extension of the similarly overgrown village green. Its legal status is, however, different as it is registered common land, though both are in the same management having been left to the National Trust with the Kingston Lacy Estate, on the death of Ralph Bankes [1981]. Freedom of public access on foot by section 29 of the National Trust Act 1907.
Registered unit CL 291.

14

COLEHILL   SZ 028 001
Leigh Common
22.77 acres, bounded on the north by the trackbed of the Southampton and
Dorchester Railway [1847] and on the south by Leigh Road. The Sir Winston
Churchill public house stands in the middle.

The pound was in the north-west corner and Leigh Pond beside the
Wimborne approach. Unfenced with mown grass near the roads and dense
wooded scrub beyond. No public right of way but a degree of informal access
takes place.

Registered unit CL 1.

COLEHILL   SU 025 010
Village Green
11 acres, crossed by unfenced roads at the heart of the village, behind the War
Memorial and opposite the distinctive European-style timber-built tower of St
Michael's Church [1893]. This large triangle of once open ground is now
virtually climax woodland with dense scrub beneath a canopy of pines.

Left to the National Trust on the death of Ralph Bankes [1981].

Registered unit VG 52.

CORFE CASTLE   SY 994 815
Ailwood Down
79.35 acres, with the best common land viewpoint panorama in Dorset, plus
18 prehistoric burial mounds along the chalk spine of the Purbeck Hills that
give their name to the adjoining Nine Barrow Down. Only nine are over two
feet high but these are superb specimens, up to ten feet high, straddling the
crest of the ridge at 600-feet above sea level.

Among the less significant mounds is the only long barrow in the Isle of
Purbeck, over collective burials of the Neolithic period, about 3500 BC.

The other mounds each covered a single urn burial, accompanied with
aristocratic grave goods and food for the after-life, being erected by the Beaker
Folk from the Rhine who established the rich warrior-dominated Wessex
culture of 2100 to 1500 BC.

Gorse scrub covers much of the hill in the vicinity of the barrow group.
The area is designated a site of special scientific interest for a negative reason,
that of the paucity of the flora. This is poor because the escarpment is
exposed to the weather and the full scorching heat of the sun.

The views are extensive in both directions. Northwards it is across the
heath and Poole Harbour to the far hills of central Dorset and Cranborne
Chase. The Swanage valley and the limestone plateau of southern Purbeck, to
the English Channel, are overlooked on the other side.

The hill is owned by the National Trust, coming to it with the estate of Ralph Bankes [1981]. It is crossed by the prehistoric ridgeway, now Corfe Castle bridleway number 17, which runs for a mile near the northern boundary. There is also a general freedom of public access on foot by section 29 of the National Trust Act 1907. Bridleway 20 extends along the entire length of the foot of the escarpment.

Registered unit CL 138.

CORFE CASTLE   SY 957 813
Corfe Common
309.1 acres, which though fenced against the A351 and the B3069, leading out of Corfe Castle towards Swanage and Kingston respectively, comprise an otherwise unenclosed landscape. It is also crossed by an unfenced public road, south from the end of West Street to Blashenwell Farm, and by east-west bridleways 36 and 30, and north-south footpaths 51, 53 and 57. Footpath 32 runs along the north-east extremity, beside Sandyhills Copse.

Corfe Common extends as a big semi-circle more than a mile wide, from the river in the west to Little Woolgarston in the east. The ponies find grassy clearings between wide sweeps of bracken and gorse. Wealden sands lie below.

The landscape is dominated by a central ridge which has been sculpted and heightened by a skyline cemetery of eight Bronze Age round barrows, dating from about 2100 to 1700 BC. They range in height from two to eight feet and are among the county's most conspicuous collections.

Mediaeval sledge-tracks are deeply gouged as overgrown cuttings through this sandy ridge. They were created during the great age of cathedral building when marble was hauled northwards, to the workshops of Corfe Castle, from the quarrylands of southern Purbeck.

Bequeathed to the National Trust on the death of the castle's last private owner, Ralph Bankes [1981]. Freedom of public access on foot by section 29 of the National Trust Act 1907.

Registered unit CL 34.

CORFE CASTLE   SY 952 843
Langton Wallis Heath
41 acres of mixed wet and dry lowland heath on the southern side of Hartland Moor National Nature Reserve, crossed by Benjamin Fayle's New Line which was a horse-drawn tramway from Norden claypits to Middlebere Jetty on Poole Harbour [1806-1905].

What is remarkable is that so little of the Dorset heaths were protected under the Commons Registration Act 1965. With the glorious exception of Holt Heath their thousands of acres slipped through the legal safety net – despite abundant living memories of their use for furze and peat fuel, cattle and pig grazing, sand and gravel digging, and the very existence of "heathcroppers" who built their cob cottage hovels from its mud and then subsisted on the surrounding landscape. Here the wetter part sustained an annual right for the removal of 2,000 turves for fuel.

This remnant passed into National Trust ownership with the estate of Ralph Bankes [1981]. Freedom of public access on foot by section 29 of the National Trust Act 1907.

Registered units CL 88 and CL 139.

CORFE CASTLE   SY 962 815
Middle Halves
17.7 acres of "The Aves" as villagers call their communal lands between West Street and East Street. Ownership unclaimed but apparently manorial waste of Corfe Castle in which case title passed to the National Trust with Ralph Bankes's huge bequest [1981]. That would give it freedom of public access – though these are hardly necessary as footpaths cross and converge from all directions – parish paths being those numbered 63, 62, 58, 57, 60 and 61.

Registered unit CL 37.

CORFE CASTLE   SZ 962 812
Town's End
9 acres, being the field on the edge of Corfe Common, between East Street and West Street at the south end of the village. Owned by the National Trust, having been bequeathed with the rest of Corfe Castle Estate on the death of Ralph Bankes [1981]. Freedom of public access on foot by section 29 of the National Trust Act 1907.

CRANBORNE and ALDERHOLT   SU 080 138
Wastelands
34.1 acres in an extensive pattern of unfenced roadside verges across the two parishes in the north-east corner of the county. Many are now wooded.

Oak and holly are the standard mix of canopy and undergrowth, with plenty of little ponds on pockets of clay.

Registered unit CL 127.

DORCHESTER   SY 698 905
Fordington Green
0.4 acres of grass, pollarded lime trees, and paths surfaced with stone-setts,
overlooked by St George's Church at the heart of Dorchester's eastern suburb.

On or beside an extensive Roman cemetery. "Not less than an hundred
skeletons" were excavated at the west end of the green, in digging the cellar
of what is now the Old Court House, next to Greenhill House [1810]. An
inscribed tombstone, to "Carinus, Roman citizen, aged 50" would be
discovered beneath the church [1907-08] and is displayed there.

St George's Fair took place annually on the green [23 April] from the
Middle Ages onwards.

Registered unit VG 4.

DORCHESTER   SY 682 912
Poundbury Camp
24.72 acres, including the ancient fortress of Poundbury (traditionally
pronounced Pummery) which was Dorchester's traditional fairground, market
place and election hustings, on a chalky green hill at the north-west corner of
the town. It is beside the road to Bradford Peverell which turns north from the
main Bridport road at the Barracks Keep. Poundbury stands above the trading
estates at the edge of the town.

The River Frome swings into the base of the hill on the north side and
has caused a precipitous slope of white, exposed chalk. The view from the top
is a localised prospect over the Frome valley which — except for an
unfortunate line of pylons staggering over the meadows — is pleasant enough.

Poundbury was an early Iron Age hill-fort refortified about AD 25 when
Maiden Castle was strengthened. It covered about twenty acres and may have
been built to protect a ford across the Frome. At any event, something is
known about this prehistoric monument as it was the scene of a small
excavation in 1939. This showed that the inner bank was originally about
thirteen feet high, its outer side faced with vertical timbers and looking down
on a V-shaped ditch thirteen feet deep. Two lines of ramparts surround three
sides of the rectangular fort, and the other, above the river, only needed one
bank because of its steepness.

This hill was the scene of one of the first preservationist battles in
Dorset, led by William Barnes, the dialect poet, who successfully stopped a
railway company slicing its line through the centre of the hill. Instead the
trains, from Weymouth to Yeovil, go under by tunnel. The land is crown
property, being part of the Prince of Wales's Dorchester estates, and is freely
open to the public "for air and exercise" under section 193 of the Law of
Property Act 1925.

This access right comes about because it is registered common land in an urban area, but like most things in Dorset even royal privileges are not to be taken for granted. When I discovered that the Duchy of Cornwall was applying to have Poundbury de-registered — upon which it would cease to be public open space — I alerted an Opposition environment spokesman, Dr David Clark MP, upon which the offending application was discreetly withdrawn to avoid the Prince further embarrassment. William Barnes would have approved.

Registered unit CL 11.

DORCHESTER and CHARMINSTER   SY 680 916
West Ward Common
113.35 acres, beside the River Frome on the bank opposite the precipitous escarpment of Poundbury Camp. These water-meadows have a network of ditches and sluices that enabled its winter inundation to protect the ground from frost and bring on a lush and early cut of hay. A second cut followed.

Grazing rights were therefore restricted to dairy cattle being turned out from 6 to 14 August and heifers and horses from 15 August to 1 November.

Right of public access "for air and exercise" under section 193 of the Law of Property Act 1925.

Registered unit CL 14.

EAST HOLME   SY 915 847
Three Lords Barrow
0.07 acres, being a low mound on a heathland knoll in western Purbeck that is notable as being the point where four parishes converge — East Holme, Arne, Church Knowle, and Steeple. It is also now on the boundary of the Lulworth Ranges, beside red flag No.43.

A piece of mediaeval church window has been planted into the three-feet high mound as a boundary stone. It probably came from the old priory church at East Holme which was an outlying cell of Cluniac monks from Montacute Abbey, Somerset. This building at East Holme was pulled down in 1746.

Behind the targets of East Holme Firing Range and out of bounds at all times even to the military. So there is no public access.

Registered unit CL 320.

EAST HOLME   SY 891 856
West Holme Heath
3.02 acres, being the north-east corner of the heath, here reclaimed for pasture, and also of the Lulworth Ranges in this part of East Holme parish. Lies beside red flag No.36. Stated to be "owned by one private owner" but

appears as Ministry of Defence property on the Army's maps. Certainly it is behind their "DANGER KEEP OUT" signs and there is no public access.

Registered unit CL 265.

EAST LULWORTH   SY 862 822
The Green

0.7 acres of trees and roadside scrub at the north end of the village, inside the triangle of roads beside Botany Wood on the B3070 at the north end of the village. Plus detached parcels of ground below the Manor House, on the Coombe Keynes road, and opposite the Weld Arms.

Registered units VG 45, VG 46 and VG 47.

EAST ORCHARD   ST 836 164
Village Pound

0.05 acres, located towards the south of this scattered Blackmore Vale community, at the road junction 150 yards east of Winchell's Farm. These two roads are tarred but the parish still has a network of green lanes that were part of an extensive drove system used for moving stock to market and for summer grazing on the chalk hills. Pounds — for impounding stray animals — are relatively common and some are protected under the Commons Registration Act 1965.

Registered unit CL 327.

EAST STOKE   SY 890 875
Ford Heath and South Heath

119.42 acres of heath and plantations, north of Binnegar Hall, to Binnegar Farm, and north-west on either side of bridleway number 16. The existence and route of this path have been disputed and a gravel grading and washing plant has been built there. There is no other public right of way.

Ancient monuments include several Bronze Age round barrows and a half-mile length of Battery Bank which was a linear defence during the insecure period that followed the collapse of Roman rule.

Registered unit CL 263.

EAST STOKE   SY 868 867
St Mary's Churchyard

0.32 acres, with ruins and gravestones in an overgrown enclosure in the meadows south of the River Frome, reached by footpath number 8 westwards from the south side of the Institute of Freshwater Ecology laboratories and then forking right along footpath 7. Moulded fragments of a fifteenth-century window and the bowl of a stoup survive. The south wall and porch were left standing when the remainder of the mediaeval church was demolished [1828]. Its replacement stands beside the main road, on the other side of the river.

Registered unit CL 266.

EAST STOKE   SY 867 875
Stokeford Common
2.9 acres of recreational allotment, north of cottage gardens beside the A352,
formerly fitted out with swings and a see-saw.
     Owned by the parish council.
     Registered unit VG 29.

EAST STOKE   SY 875 870
Village Pound
0.05 acres, on the south side of the A352.
     Registered unit CL 126.

FIFEHEAD NEVILLE   ST 755 110
Deadmoor Common
103 acres of formerly open land, almost entirely engulfed in dense scrub, on
clay soil at the heart of the Blackmore Vale. Flat and low-lying, it is squelchy
for much of the year. At the hub of an intricate network of green lanes and
droveways, extending from the escarpment of the Dorset Downs to the
market towns of Sturminster Newton and Shaftesbury, it would once have
been the focal point for stock moving over a wide distance.

     Now it is the biggest unofficial nature reserve in north Dorset. The
vegetation is a mix of blackthorn, sallow, mature oaks and coarse grass, in that
order of magnitude though in places all four overlap into a single
impenetrable habitat. Some birch creeps into the tree-line around the
occasional clearings. Here you startle the jays which are the typical bird of oak
woodlands.

     Indeed you are liable to disturb roe deer or anything as this is among the
wildest places in Dorset.

     Access is down a dank hollow, narrow and double hedged, north-west
from the tiny hamlet of Woodrow. This lies a mile and a half south-west of
Sturminster Newton.

     You leave the A357, southwards, at the "Fifehead Neville" turn, opposite
the Red Lion.

     Look out for Woodrow House. Opposite is the thatched Elm Tree
Cottage and Hambledon bungalow. From them an untarred track, legally a
public road, bends to the right and descends to the outer tongue of Deadmoor
Common. Here the path widens into grassland. Fifehead Neville footpath
number 1 turns to the right and runs for half a mile just inside the eastern
boundary of the common — though you seldom glimpse the fence-line —
northwards to Holbrook Lane and Lydlinch.

     Straight on from the initial clearing, Fifehead Neville footpath number 4
goes west for a quarter of a mile, and then leaves the common to enter

Brakethorne Copse. Both paths are kept open by horse-riders and liable to be exceedingly muddy. For much of the year this is gumboot country — and in midwinter you may well sink in to the tops of your Wellingtons.

Registered unit CL 43.

FIFEHEAD NEVILLE ST 779 117
Higher Fifehead Common
4 acres of grass and woody scrub, along a low ridge in the north-east corner of the parish, above the valley of the River Divelish. It probably owes its survival to duplications in the local lane system, particularly as both parallel routes have been tarred.

Approached from the A357 via Rivers Corner, in the Newton hamlet of Sturminster Newton, to the north. The eastern lane climbs the hill from The Common — enclosed and extinct — at Okeford Fitzpaine. The third road on to the hill is from the south-west, from a picturesque ford and packhorse bridge at Fifehead.

Westwards, from the central of the three junctions on Higher Fifehead Common, extends Fifehead Neville bridleway number 11, which descends to Plumber Manor.

Registered unit CL 329.

FRAMPTON SY 626 949
Flower Bed
0.03 acres roadside flower garden beside the A356 at the junction beside the parish church, overlooked by an attractive row of Sheridan estate almshouses.

Owned by the parish council.

Registered unit VG 68.

FROME ST QUINTIN ST 607 020
Poor Allotment
19.22 acres of high chalk downland, west of Long Ash Lane — now the A37 — without any public right of way. It lies some distance up from the village, such is the lot of the poor, but has almost easy access compared with the allotments above Sydling St Nicholas.

Registered unit CL 169.

GILLINGHAM ST 820 298
Forest Deer Leases
32 acres, being a fenced rectangle of grassland that was at the heart of the mediaeval Gillingham Forest. It was hunted by King John from King's Court Palace, the earthworks of which lie beside the semi-modern railway line about two miles south.

The Deer Leases are crossed by Gillingham public footpath 12. This is reached via the B3098, midway between Gillingham and Mere.

Turn east at Mapperton Hill Farm, on to a mile-long cul-de-sac lane which passes Huntingford and then beds south to Forest Side Farm. From this corner you walk north-east, avoiding another path which goes straight ahead, and the Deer Leases are the third field.

Registered unit CL 31.

GODMANSTONE ST 666 113
Church Lane

0.05 acres, near the parish church. Roadside setting rather than usable village green.

Registered unit VG 9.

HAMPRESTON SZ 046 998
Little Canford Common

0.37 acres, next to the lane from Hampreston village to the Fox Inn, between it and the River Stour. The road converges with a bend in the river between Stourbank Nurseries and Manor Farm.

Registered unit CL 134.

HILTON ST 771 037
Ansty Cross

0.85 acres of dense hillside woodland beside the central element of the collection of Ansty junctions that are the hub of the lane system in the heart of the Dorset Downs. Created by a triangle of mediaeval roads, though the north-west side is now a public path, Hilton footpath 34.

Registered until CL 353.

HOLT SU 031 032
God's Blessing Green

3.3 acres of roadside verges between Colehill and Holt, with the charm of a fine name and a suitably rustic setting. This includes a thatched timber-framed seventeenth century farmhouse.

Former Bankes estate land which passed to the National Trust [1981]. Freedom of public access on foot by section 29 of the National Trust Act 1907.

Registered unit CL 80.

HOLT SU 039 055
Holt Forest

174.6 acres, being the major surviving remnant of mediaeval royal hunting ground north of Holt village, providing fuel and clearings for eighteenth century cottagers.

Crossed by three unfenced lanes east of Little Lodge Farm. Penetrated by a series of footpaths (numbered 42, 46, 47 and 51) and bridleways (43, 44, 45, 48 and 63). Came into National Trust ownership with the Kingston Lacy Estate on the death of Ralph Bankes [1981]. Managed by English Nature as a National Nature Reserve. Freedom of public access on foot by section 29 of the National Trust Act 1907.

Registered unit CL 19.

HOLT   SU 058 040
Holt Heath National Nature Reserve

1,057.7 acres, comprising almost all of Holt Heath apart from the Driver's Plantation beside White Sheet Hill, of special note for being by far the biggest block of common land in Dorset. Already leased to the Nature Conservancy Council, now English Nature, it passed into National Trust ownership with the bequest of Ralph Bankes's even greater estate [1981].

The Bronze Age Bull Barrow lies on the ridge above the Mannington Brook. The Bee Garden, half a mile south, is a rectangular enclosure with banks three feet high amid a group of larger enclosures that covered a hundred acres.

It may be quite ancient and the apiary that provided its name could have been the later use for which the convenient clearing was put. There was still subsistence farming carried out on the heath until about 1800, mainly from White House Holdings; the mud walls from this have since crumbled to almost nothing.

The extensive area of heath and gorse north of Forestry Commission plantations provide a refuge for the Dartford warbler and are the last thin corridor of wild lands that still link the Dorset heaths with those of the New Forest.

Crossed in the northern part by numerous footpaths (numbered 1, 2, 22, 21, 23, 5, 6 and 7) and with sparser access to the much bigger southern part. Here it is crossed by bridleways (numbered 25, 62, 19, 11, 13, 14 and 15) plus footpaths 12 and 10, the latter having its boggy moments. General freedom of public access on foot by section 29 of the National Trust Act 1907.

Registered unit CL 21.

HOLT   SU 040 060
Holt Wood

35.17 acres of manorial waste of the manor of Holt, which belonged to the manor of Kingston Lacy and passed with the rest of its estate to the National Trust [1981]. Somewhat fragmented arms of ancient woodland encroached upon by the cottages of post-mediaeval heathcroppers.

Crossed by footpaths numbered 50, 51 and 52, which intersect. Freedom of public access on foot by section 29 of the National Trust Act 1907.

Registered unit CL 18.

HOLT   SU 029 038
Village Green

4 acres, in a large triangle of sloping grass opposite the school and Vicarage Farm at the centre of this widely scattered community. It was the venue for the mediaeval James Farm, held on St James's Day [25 July]. The principal botanical interest lies in the soggy area towards the bottom, where it is crossed by footpath number 39.

Came into National Trust ownership with the Kingston Lacy estate [1981].

Registered unit VG 6.

HOLWELL   ST 716 114
Peaceful Lane

4.62 acres of exceedingly wide roadside verge, which is a mile long, from Packers Hill to Woodbridge, with a cottage attractively positioned midway along. These are the low clay soils of the Blackmore Vale and it can be subject to flooding. Typical lowland droveway; well named and would be even more charming if it were a green lane rather than a tarred public road.

Registered unit CL 340.

HORTON   SU 080 070
Horton Common

53.15 acres, being the north-east corner of what was formerly several hundred acres of heath. The registered area is bounded by footpath 21, from Horton Farm, and bridleway 7 to the south. It is crossed by footpath 8. Bridleway 7 turns north to follow the dismantled railway that cuts it off from the rest of the now "improved" heath.

Registered unit CL 122.

HORTON   SU 063 071
Horton Heath

28 acres, claimed as a fragmented part of the former Horton Common. The registered area is north of Bog Farm and has no public rights of way. Monmouth Ash, where the Duke of Monmouth was discovered hiding in a ditch after the Battle of Sedgemoor [1685], lies a couple of fields to the west.

Registered unit CL 16.

HORTON and WOODLANDS
Haythorn Common

SU 037 077

9.4 acres either side of the unfenced section of the lane at Haythorn. The north-west arm, beside Haythorn Copse, led to Marland Pit. Footpath number 29 heads south east, beyond the chapel.

Registered unit CL 17.

HURN
Sopley Common

SZ 135 975

91.4 acres of wild heathland, peat bogs, and woods either side of the western section of the Avon Causeway. Having been lost from the parish of Sopley to that of Hurn, the land has consequently been removed from Hampshire to Dorset.

That said, it still had numerous claimants, with 31 registered rights of turbary, 29 of estovers, 23 to shoot rabbit and duck, three simply to shoot, and one each for a range of activities including the removal of tree loppings, gorse, and a single Christmas tree.

Footpath number 28 strikes off north, from the west side of the bridge across the A338, and bridleway 7 joins the Avon Causeway from the south.

Registered unit CL 26.

IBBERTON
Back Hollow

ST 790 075

0.6 acres of scrubby chalk escarpment, immediately overlooking the hillside church steps and the parish church itself, which are set into the side of the ridge at the top end of the village. The land is at the junction of the halter path — a publicly maintained road — and the steep tarred lane that climbs to Baker's Folly and on to Bulbarrow Hill.

Registered unit CL 352.

IWERNE MINSTER
Chalk Crossroads

ST 867 143

0.12 acres of tree ring landscaping that enhances the lower junction in this fully-thatched village of banded flint and stone cottages.

Registered unit CL 29.

IWERNE MINSTER
Church Road

ST 868 144

0.12 acres of tree ring at the junction just south of the parish church. Villagers were vigilant in protecting every fragment of their exquisite setting.

Registered unit CL 30.

IWERNE MINSTER ST 893 143
Lime Pits
3.92 acres of Cranborne Chase woodland at the western end of Stubhampton valley, nearly three miles from Iwerne Minster village. Here the ground was dug for the production of lime-mortar and marl for the clay fields of the vale villages.

Beside the road into the valley, 800 yards east of Hill Farm, at its junction with bridleway number 23.

Registered unit CL 209.

IWERNE MINSTER ST 867 145
The War Office
0.12 acres at the junction in the centre of the village, alternatively named "the News Office" — another echo of the Great War. Initially the parish pump canopy, open sided beneath a tiled roof, was furnished with notice boards as the 1914 conflict failed to be over by Christmas.

These panels soon filled with news, postcards and photographs, attracting growing attention as the news from the Western Front became grimmer and local casualties mounted. By the end of the war these hoardings had been provided with a purpose-built stone shelter, the War Office, lined with displays and open fronted beneath a lamp and a winged angel.

From December 1917, in return for the information being sent to him by the combatants, estate owner James Hainsworth Ismay began the three-weekly *Iwerne Times* for those serving overseas. This gave the pastoral news, such as hog-sale prices, hurdle-making in the coppices, and the visiting "Buy War Savings Certificates" film. From abroad came information on prisoners of war. The sting was at the start: "I'm afraid my first news to you must be sad, for it will tell you of deaths of your friends."

Registered unit CL 111.

LEIGH ST 614 097
Bere Hill Mead
1.65 acres of pasture beside footpath number 7 which leaves the tarred lane 100 yards south of Stake Ford Cross, which is another reminder of communal customs. Suicides were traditionally buried at night, beside a crossroads on the parish boundary, with a stake through their heart to lay the ghost.

Registered unit CL 93.

LEIGH ST 631 088
Higher Totnell
0.57 acre wooded plot opposite Higher Totnell Farm, beside Bailey Ridge road at its junction with byway number 18.

Registered unit CL 92.

LEIGH   ST 626 078

Long Bridge Drove

0.95 acre stream-side plot immediately north of central section of the drove,
which is byway number 20.

    Registered unit CL 94.

LONG BURTON   ST 655 113

Burton Common

56.4 acres of coarse grass, bullrushes, and low scrub in the almost flat south-
east corner of the parish, extending from the A352 to The Cam stream.
Enclosed against the main road and its perimeter. Grazed by horses and cattle
and crossed, along the north side, by bridleway number 11.

    Registered unit CL 6.

LYDLINCH   ST 736 136

Lydlinch Common

70 acres, forming the archetypal southern English common. Several
farmsteads face on to what is the only substantial vestige of mediaeval open
landscape to survive in the Blackmore Vale. The effect is magnified by the fact
that two main roads cross it and come to a busy junction.

    These are the A357, from Sturminster Newton to Stalbridge, and the
A3030, westwards towards Sherborne. Their junction is beside an area of
spongy grass that is still grazed by cattle. Elsewhere the extensive scrub
becomes a great drift of white flower when the "blackthorn winter" heralds
the spring. These bushes are home to one of the largest colonies of
nightingales in the country.

    Westwards is climax woodland, pressing in from Stock Wood and
Brickles Wood, of ancient vintage. It is one of the few Wessex locations to
have the occasional wild service tree, unplanted by man and an indicator of
species of a remnant of the primaeval forest canopy.

    At the other extreme, on the eastern extremity, are jubilee and
coronation commemorative oaks. Here the common is more like a village
green and overshadowed by the church tower. "Lydlinch bells be good vor
zound," wrote William Barnes, "and hear by volks vor miles around."

    As well as the two roads, the common is intersected by Lydlinch public
footpaths 27 and 23, and has a custom of de facto public access. Despite the
main roads the grazing of cattle has continued on a limited scale, behind
electric fences, and there are occasional appearances of traditional-style
gypsies with horse and caravan.

    Registered unit CL 42.

LYTCHETT MATRAVERS   SY 954 952
Elder Rise
0.85 acres of unfenced scrubby heath on the edge of Elder Moor, beside the western end of Huntick Road, north-west of Huntick Farm. Reputedly haunted by a spectral hearse, which may well have been a creation of smugglers on one of their key routes inland from Poole Harbour.
Registered unit CL 297.

MARNHULL   ST 767 181
Recreational Allotment
3.3 acres playing field just above the Stour meadows, west of Pope's Farm and Pleck in the south-west corner of this sprawling village.
Registered unit VG 28.

MARSHWOOD   SY 363 987
Lambert's Castle Plain
10.62 acres of unfenced top-land, at the 750-feet contour south-west of Lambert's Castle Hill and the site of its admiralty Telegraph Station [1806-22] and its annual fair and racecourse circuit [1709-1947]. This inland eminence above the Marshwood Vale, midway between Crewkerne and Lyme Regis, was transferred from Devon to Dorset in the 1960s, and is owned by the National Trust. Freedom of public access on foot.

There is a typical common-land look to the open south-west parts, with the hilltop triangle of registered common being delineated by the B3165 and the lane to Fishpond, with footpath number 72 along the third side. Patches of gorsy heath are interspersed with tussocks of *Molina caerulea*, the purple moor grass, in a piece of relict scenery that was painted by Lucien Pissarro [1863-1944] and James Manson [1879-1945]. The former had a cottage in Fishpond Bottom and the two corresponded and visited each other for 35 years.
Registered unit CL 234.

MELBURY ABBAS   ST 900 196
Melbury Wood
197 acres, otherwise known as Breeze Hill and Melbury Hill, forming the northern backdrop to the National Trust's Melbury Down holding — the deep-cut chalkland combe through the heights of Cranborne Chase between Compton Abbas Airfield and Win Green. Visual access only, from the Trust's grassy slopes to the south, as there are no public paths through what are now dense mixed plantations.
Registered unit CL 212.

MILBORNE ST ANDREW

SY 796 978

Parish Pit

0.1 acres of landscaped mediaeval chalk-pit, beside the junction of the Dewlish road out of the village and Milborne St Andrew bridleway number 18, at Springfields. Chalk blocks were widely used for building in the Dorset Downs and though now almost invariably rendered with concrete on cottage walls, "raw" vernacular examples have survived into recent times in this valley, on the hillside and beside the public road to Brook Farm and Dewlish Mill.

Registered unit CL 100.

MORDEN

SY 914 955

Churchland Green

0.1 acres, with the war memorial obelisk at the corner, beside the road junction and Church Villa in East Morden village. Crossed by footpath number 10, on the west side of New Lane.

Owned by the parish council.

Registered unit VG 26.

NETHER COMPTON

SY 598 173

The Green

1 acre of grass and trees in the centre of the village, between the parish church and footpath number 14.

Registered unit VG 38.

OKEFORD FITZPAINE

ST 808 108

Greenhayes

0.3 acres of token grass beside the village hall, though formerly the green was in the triangle formed by the roads at the centre of the village, which became a poorhouse in 1837. The present green fails to be as attractive as its location might suggest, though it is at least accessible with a public road on one side and footpath number 53 on the other. Owned by the parish council.

Registered unit VG 18.

PAMPHILL

ST 992 044 and 997 025

Hinton Moor and Pilsmoor

180.15 acres, made up of two detached sets of water-meadows on the west side of the Allen valley. Hinton Moor is opposite Hinton Mill, Hinton Parva, and Pilsmoor is below Stanbridge. The latter meadows are touched by footpath 30, north from High Hall to Stanbridge, but there are no other public rights of way to either area.

Registered unit CL 60.

PAMPHILL   ST 974 021 to 984 049
King Down
271.25 acres of former unfenced sheep range, put under the plough as a result
of wartime agricultural regulations [1940] and still partly under intensive
agriculture. Passed with the Bankes estate into National Trust ownership
[1981], giving that body something of a dilemma under its own statutory
requirements for the care of common land.

Some grassland has been restored. There are also two Bronze Age burial
mounds, dating to the Wessex culture between 2100 and 1600 BC, but two
others in this group were totally eradicated by ploughing.

Crossed by a network of public paths, with footpath number 19 beside
Lodge Farm – a genuine mediaeval hunting lodge – at the south, and footpath
26 leaving the Kingston Lacy estate, for Witchampton, in the north. Bridleway
number 21 runs almost the entire two-mile length of the common, north from
the east end of the Beech Avenue [planted 1835], and bridleways 24 and 25
form east-west links in the middle.

Badbury Rings is to the west and the huge Bradford Barrow is just off the
Trust's land to the north.

Registered unit CL 70.

PAMPHILL   ST 990 008
Pamphill Green
29.9 acres, including a Bronze Age round barrow in the southern extremity.
This is called Little Pamphill and faces a row of thatched cottages and the Vine
Inn. The cottages of Pamphill are mainly cob and thatch and were built on
common land by the exercise of one year's squatters' rights.

More substantially, facing the junction at the middle of the green, is a
range of neat William and Mary brickwork almshouses and school buildings
combined under one roof. These were the gift of Roger Gillingham in 1698 "to
God and ye poor".

To the north there is a perfect idyll of the English village green, cricket
included, with St Stephen's Church in the leafy canopy beyond. Unfenced
lanes skirt through tongues of the green and there is no main road traffic to
spoil the tranquility. An avenue of oaks was planted in 1846 and the rustic,
thatched cricket pavilion added in 1907. It is a delightful, semi-modern
contribution to this mediaeval dream-land. The scene is marred only by the
unfortunate coincidence that 160-feet pylons of the National Grid march
down into the Stour valley at this point, though, given that National Trust
ownership is in perpetuity, perhaps something may eventually be done to
remove them.

Part of the former Bankes estate and now owned by the National Trust.
Registered unit VG 8.

PENTRIDGE
SU 033 178
Village Green

0.7 acres, being a typical chalkland village green. Its open grass is dominated by the spire of St Rumbold's Church — claiming the first known forefather of poet Robert Browning — and flint-built cottages. Public rights also converge, in the form of bridleways number 1, 2 and 3. Owned by the Official Custodian for Charities.

Registered unit VG 1.

PIMPERNE
ST 903 095
Cross Piece

0.07 acres of what might more properly be regarded as former village green, beside the church gate and mediaeval preaching cross. Previously used for mounting one's horse and now for parking. Notable for its associations with Charles Kingsley who was curate at Pimperne before the onset of fame.

Nervously restless and vacillating from intense depression into repressed paedophilia, he would turn that frustration into a classic, *The Water Babies* [1863].

Registered unit CL 210.

POOLE
SY 995 974
Barrow Hill

28.35 acres, containing the best preserved and most conspicuous prehistoric cemetery of the eastern Dorset heaths. Six skyline burial mounds are classic Bronze Age Wessex Culture specimens; four being of the "bell" type with a berm between the mound and the surrounding ditch.

Three were dug by Victorian antiquary John Austen, who found urns with the primary cremations and later inhumations which had been disposed towards the tops of existing mounds.

They vary in height, up to eight feet, and are set on the plateau at the top of the ridge at about 200 feet above sea level. Date 2100 to 1500 BC.

Their landscape is also an ecological remant of some note, with the full range of lowland heath diversity — from trees and gorse scrub, through sandy heather slopes, down to peat bog and sallow bushes in Rushcombe Bottom. It sustains relict colonies of sand lizards and smooth snakes; plus Dartford Warblers breeding in the old gorse.

Northwards are Cogdean Elms and Happy Bottom, Corfe Mullen, on the mixed soils towards the Stour meadows. The southern side, beyond Rushcombe Bottom has more heather clumps, co-existing with the golf course and school on Corfe Hills, with the houses of Broadstone beyond. Together they form the Corfe and Barrow Hills site of special scientific interest.

The west side is flanked by the straight line of bridleway number 1, which is three dimensional in places as it is the raised causeway of the Roman road from Badbury Rings to Hamworthy. Crossed by footpath 2 and having a general right of public access "for air and exercise" under section 193 of the Law of Property Act 1925.

Registered unit CL 233.

POOLE   SZ 024 922
Gorsehill Common

1.52 acres, aptly named, being a hilltop tangle of gorse, brambles, bracken, a few birch and other trees, and some clumps of garden-escape bluebells. It must be the best hedgehog and fox reserve of the inner conurbation.

House and rooftop views plus a glimpse of the harbour. Beside an unsigned track from between numbers 70 and 72 Pound Lane, which leads to St Mary's Roman Catholic School, in Devon Road. There is no access from Gorse Hill Road.

Crossed by a network of unofficial paths and having a general right of public access "for air and exercise" under section 193 of the Law of Property Act 1925.

Registered unit CL 223.

PORTLAND   SY 645 778 to 677 683
Chesil Beach to Portland Bill

238.65 acres extending virtually the whole length of the western side of the parish and island, from the windswept pebbles of the Chesil Beach to the rocky southern tip of Dorset. Broken only by unregistered scree slopes at West Weares and Blacknor headland.

Also extends around the north-east side of the Bill to Red Crane, Cellar's Ledge, Longpoints, Broad Ope, and Cave Hole. Stretches intermittently inland beside the Lawnsheds, as the island's unfenced strip-fields are known. Then resumes north of Cheyne Weares and around Church Ope Cove, with beach-huts between the precipitons crags and the shingle beach.

Islanders registered rights to do just about anything possible with the land – turning out any livestock within the description "Animals"; removal of stone and pebbles; lifting turf; sea fishing; estovers to include sea-borne debris and picking up dry cow dung for fuel.

Owned by the Crown Estates Commissioners. Rights held by the Commoners and Court Leet of the Island and Royal Manor of Portland. General right of public access "for air and exercise" under section 193 of the Law of Property Act 1925.

Registered unit CL 2.

PORTLAND   SY 670 755

Harbour Shore

26.12 acres beside the A354 approach road on the west side of Portland Harbour. Includes the thrift-covered embankment of the island's former branch railway [1865-1965] and extends north as the tongue of land that reaches the Small Mouth passage into The Fleet lagoon.

Usual wide-ranging Portland rights were claimed by commoners, and there is a general right of public access "for air and exercise" under section 193 of the Law of Property Act 1925.

Registered unit CL 71.

PORTLAND   SY 685 712

Roadside Verges

43.52 acres of "land and verges along minor roads around Weston and Easton" which are the main villages on the top of the island. Many of these roads are unfenced and the roadsides wide, extending in parts to include areas of quarry waste.

The same blanket rights were registered as for the Chesil Beach, including piscary potential – in Easton Pond, perhaps – and there is also a general right of public access "for air and exercise" under section 193 of the Law of Property Act 1925.

Registered unit CL 72.

PORTLAND   SY 690 733

Verne Yeates

26.12 acres of spectacular hillside, including the viewpoint car-parks overlooking Fortuneswell and the Chesil Beach. Climbed by footpath number 4, which is the Old Hill ascent on to the top of the island. Footpath 76 comes up further east, from Castletown, along the dismantled Merchants' Railway [1826-1940]. This was an incline-operated narrow gauge line which carried stone.

Footpath 85 and Yeates Road, which becomes Glacis, run the length of the hilltop – at 375 feet above sea level. Open space begins around the war memorial above Priory Corner, opposite Portland Heights Hotel, and extends for just about as far as you can physically go. Downhill is difficult and eastwards you hit legal retrainsts.

There is a right of public access "for air and exercise" under section 193 of the Law of Property Act of 1925, extending as far as the "NO UNAUTHORISED ENTRY" notice on the wall of Verne Citadel, which is now Her Majesty's Prison.

Registered unit CL 4.

PORTESHAM

SY 603 857

The Green

0.1 acres of grass and ornamental trees, plus a covered well, facing Front Street beside the bend in the B3157 as it passes through the village.

Owned by the parish council.

Registered unit VG 3.

POWERSTOCK

SY 538 956

Poor Mead Common

1.32 acres in the deep-cut valley between King's Farm and Luccas Farm.

Owned by the trustees for the poor of the parish. There are no public rights of way.

Registered unit CL 25.

PUNCKNOWLE

SY 534 884

Knacker's Hole

2.47 acres of rough grass, scrub and trees in the hollow to the south of the village that is climbed by footpath number 26.

Registered unit CL 9.

ST LEONARDS AND ST IVES

SU 122 046

Ashley Heath Recreation Ground

4.3 acres, given to the parish council by John Evans and John Elmore. Beside Horton Road with housing estates all around. Some heathland flora survives, including pines and birch, with gorse and heather below. Footpath number 19 enters at the south end, from St Ives.

Registered unit VG 95.

ST LEONARDS AND ST IVES

SU 133 023 and SZ 133 043

Leybrook Common

21 acres, of which 18.83 acres of heath and pines have travelled across the map and can now be found on the north-east slopes of Matchams View picnic area in Avon Country Park. Its legal existence began as part of Town Common and Sopley Common, in the parishes of Christchurch and Hurn, where the Department of Transport requisitioned common land for the building of the A338 "Spur Road" from Ringwood to Bournemouth [1967].

17.2 acres was acquired by the road builders and provided in its place, as "exchange land". This comprised roadside verge and a dense pinewood on the east side of the big Ashley Heath roundabout.

There some 13 acres remain, as a wide grassy anti-noise bund against the busy main road. The remainder was exchanged for a second time — by owners Dorset County Council — for Matchams View, which was already public access land [1992].

This was to enable the sale of the Ashley Heath pinewood for house building to developer Barrie Price at a figure upwards of £200,000. Exchange land was necessary under section 147 of the Inclosure Act 1845.

The Secretary of State for the Environment upheld the deal and agreed to move most of the common, for a second time, despite objections: "The Open Spaces Society noted that although the exchange land was more than three times larger than the common land, the former was already public open space, and it was not the society's policy to accept land already open to the public in exchange for historically important common land."

Quite how historically significant is questionable, given that the previous Leybrook Common was created by a road scheme, but the way it has moved around the countryside may well be unique – this is Dorset's phantom common.

Registered unit CL 294.

ST LEONARDS AND ST IVES   SU 103 040
Lions Hill
30.77 acres of woods and heather on the western side of Ashley Heath. Lions Hill Farm is to the west and the "Old Road" of Castleman's Corkscrew to the north. Charles Castleman's railway [1847-1964] is now a cycleway.

Registered unit CL 237.

ST LEONARDS AND ST IVES   SU 135 047
Old Town Pits
6.27 acres of disused sand and gravel workings beside the B3081, including the Old Gravel Pit which was subject to separate registration. They are set in the slope beside the A31, 500 yards north-east of Ashley Heath roundabout. Footpath number 3 goes through the pits – their "Town" name refers to Ringwood, a mile away on the far bank of the River Avon.

Registered unit CL 91 and CL 236.

SHAFTESBURY and CANN   ST 854 225 to 844 203
Breach Common and St James's Common
86 acres, including the square parcel of overgrown Breach Common, at Alcester below Shaftesbury's western slope, fanning out into the most extensive network of common land road verges in Dorset. Rushy in places, on heavy clay soils, these extend for a total of three miles

They are cropped annually for hay and traditionally visited by the Cooper family of gypsies. The system can be followed by car along tarred public roads, west from the St James district of lower Shaftesbury to Edwards Farm and Cherry Orchard Farm, towards Stour Row.

36

The verges are at their widest in the triangular areas created by road junctions, such as here and to the south-east, on the other side of Cole's Lane Farm. The extensive St James's Common then splays to spread tentacles on both sides of Guy's Marsh Youth Custody Centre.

The main arm runs to the east, via Holm Farm and Ivy Farm and then south to the southern extremity of the parish of Cann. The lesser option heads west of the detention centre, with an offshoot stretching further west to Little London and Paynthouse Farm.

There is open access from all the country lanes and a legal right of access "for air and exercise" under section 193 of the Law of Property Act 1925, across Breach Common which is also intersected by Shaftesbury public footpaths number 36 and 37.

Registered unit CL 41.

SHERBORNE ST 620 152
Lenthay Common

57.17 acres of grazing land west of the town. In the eighteenth century it was known as The Moor and included a racecourse more than a mile in length. This was later converted to a golf course, which ceased at the end of the Edwardian era [1911].

The area at the end of Lenthay Road was called The Green and had the town's cricket pitch.

Here the grass conceals the site of an extensive Roman villa which lies just west of footpath number 1, with other rooms on the far side of the railway line. A mosaic of a naked Apollo, playing the lyre with a double-fluted Marsyas prancing in front of him, was excavated and removed [1836]. It is reset in the floor of the Dairy House at Sherborne Castle.

Lenthay Common (pronounced "Lenthee") is crossed by footpath number 3, westwards to Silverlake Farm, and there is a general right of public access "for air and exercise" under section 193 of the Law of Property Act 1925.

Registered unit CL 24.

SHILLINGSTONE ST 850 103
Hodmoor

2.62 acres of idyllic meadows on the east bank of the River Stour, overlooked from the other side of the water by the wooded precipice beside the Iron Age hill-fort of Hod Hill. Part of the flood-plain of the river with its traditional inundations keeping the frost off the ground and bringing on early crops of grass.

The river is particularly slow and wide as it flows between the contrasting landscapes of flat meadows on one side and the sheer hillside on the other. Approached by a publicly maintained cul-de-sac road eastwards from the A357, the turning on the humped summit of Gain's Cross, but without any public rights of way along the riverbank.

Registered unit CL 76.

SHILLINGSTONE   ST 827 103
Puzzle Drove
1 acre of lane-grass beside footpath number 31 on the south edge of the village, between White Pit and the road to the huge modern chalk quarry in the side of Shillingstone Hill. Part of an extensive network of green lane droveways between the chalk escarpment and the market town of Sturminster Newton — very few of which had their common grazing rights claimed.

Registered unit CL 341.

SHILLINGSTONE   ST 824 114
Village Cross
0.05 acres of A357 roadside grass at the site of the village maypole, which survived until the 1930s, and still dominated by the attractively restored Hamstone cross. Owned by the parish council.

Registered unit VG 10.

SILTON   ST 779 302
Stroud Common
2 acres, south of Bourton and its A303 bypass, on the west side of Silton village hall, at the top of the slope above Stour Bridge. The rest of the former Stroud Common is now enclosed fields but this remnant was retained for public recreational use. It is owned by the parish council.

Registered unit VG 31.

SIXPENNY HANDLEY   ST 956 166
Minchington Cross
0.2 acres triangle of grass beside a railed clump of beech trees at the junction of the B3081 and Oakley Lane, in a picturesque valley east of Tollard Royal. Northwards, an avenue leads towards Rushmore House, into the coppices of Cranborne Chase and the county of Wiltshire.

Registered unit CL 200.

STALBRIDGE   ST 737 176
The Ring
0.2 acres, being the village green towards the southern end of the former market town of Stalbridge. Unfenced and triangular, with roads on each side. The main road is the A357 to Sturminster Newton.

Owned by the parish council, it has the Victorian pumps for this part of town, plus a flagpole. Formal flower-beds make it look rather suburbanised.

Things were not always so. Lucy Taylor, who died in 1947, recounted a "skimmington riding" procession of the type described by Thomas Hardy in *The Mayor of Casterbridge*. These were a communal display of outrage against transgressions of the moral code. In the Stalbridge case local people paraded with sacking over their heads and beat saucepans with tongs and spoons. They assembled around a conveyance carrying caricatures of the guilty pair. The effigies were then burnt at The Ring.

Overlooking the green, on the east side, are a row of ten stone and slate town-houses that were built in about 1825. Known as Anglesey Cottages, they perpetuate the link between the town and the Annesley family whose head, the Marquis of Anglesey, wrote to me in 1969 about an incident in which an ancestor's life had been saved here. The Ring is owned by the parish council.

Registered unit VG 2.

STOCKWOOD   ST 589 075
Stockwood Common
9.92 acres of wide roadside verges along the lane above Church Farm, to the thatched Manor Farm. Stockwood hamlet lies below, with an exquisite wooded backdrop that provided Thomas Hardy with his main "Hintock" setting for the novel The *Woodlanders* [1887].

Registered unit CL 84.

STOKE ABBOTT   ST 433 014
Burstock Down
6.57 acres, wooded in part, on the western foothills of Lewesdon Hill. On the south side of Lewesdon Hill Lane, now bridleway number 8, at the 650 feet contour. Its views are northwards, over Broadwindsor.

Registered unit CL 68.

STOURPAINE   ST 863 088
Stour Slopes
1.52 acres of grass and blackthorn hillside rising from the east bank of the River Stour immediately north of Durweston Bridge. On the west side of the A350 road, between Blandford and Shaftesbury, and crossed by the cutting of the Somerset and Dorset Railway. This was formally opened on 31 August 1863 and fell to Dr Richard Beeching's axe, with its last passenger train running from Bournemouth West Station to Bath on 6 March 1966.

The land, which is steeply sloped, has a dense hedgerow beside the busy main road and there are no public rights of way.

Registered unit CL 246.

STUDLAND
The Green

SZ 033 824

0.2 acres of grass and specimen trees, opposite the village hall at the crossroads of Heath Green Road and School Lane with the main Swanage road. Owned by the National Trust and overlooked by a row of modern cottages, in red brick with dormers, which won acclaim for architect Alexander Hamilton-Fletcher [1991].
Registered unit VG 37.

STURMINSTER MARSHALL
The Pound

ST 951 003

0.02 acres beside the churchyard, off Church Street, with easy access to water at the nearby River Stour.
Registered unit CL 173.

STURMINSTER MARSHALL
Johnny's Ditch

ST 948 003

0.05 acres, comprising a hollow on the north-west side of the village, beside the Stour meadows.
Registered unit CL 252.

STURMINSTER MARSHALL
Trafalgar Green

ST 951 003

0.01 acres of post-protected grass at a road junction in the village.
Owned by the parish council.
Registered unit VG 42.

STURMINSTER MARSHALL
Village Green

ST 950 002

0.3 acres, in two unfenced triangles of grass at the centre of this large village. Full of historical associations, including the Market Place street-name — a memory of rights granted by the Earl of Pembroke in 1101 — and the stocks which were last used in 1860 and now replaced [1986].

Pride of place went to the last maypole to survive in Dorset, erected by Charles Parke of Henbury House to celebrate Queen Victoria's golden jubilee, when an oak was planted nearby [1887]. This pine pole decayed and has now been replaced with a new maypole, topped by a weather-vane in the shape of a water vole, which is the village symbol.
Owned by the parish council.
Registered unit VG 40.

SUTTON WALDRON   ST 884 163
Sutton Clump
1.35 acres, dominated by fir trees, on the west side of the Higher Blandford Road, midway between Blandford and Shaftesbury. Here a country lane heads west, at the 680-feet contour, to cross the lip of the escarpment of Cranborne Chase and descend into the Blackmore Vale.

The parcel of hill land is in the triangle formed by the main road on the west side and the fork of the lane to Sutton Waldron. This gives its alternative local name of Gore Clump; 'gore' being the old name for a triangular piece of land.

Sutton Clump is on Sutton Hill. Confusingly there is a second Gore Clump, a mile and a half to the north — and also triangular — beside Compton Abbas Airfield.

Registered unit CL 205.

SYDLING ST NICHOLAS   SY 652 985
The Poorlots
18.62 acres of high downland — now a mix of grass, scrub and woods — two miles south-east of the village. This is the far corner of the parish, and to reach these allotments the poor had an uphill walk.

The land they were allocated is on the steep and exposed west-facing slope of Ridge Hill, below bridleway number 5 which runs along the east side. Charity did not begin at home; their location and terrain must have seemed a poor joke.

Owned by the parish council.

Registered unit CL 171.

SYMONDSBURY   SY 440 925
Eype Down
120.65 acres of hilly bracken and scrub above Down House Farm, inland from Thorncombe Beacon, with dramatic views across to Golden Cap and Colmer's Hill. Crossed by bridleway number 39 south from Quarr Cross on the A35, and footpath 42 from the north-east corner of the common at the top end of Higher Eype Road.

Offshoot footpath number 40 drops down into National Trust land and number 43 heads the other way, towards Lower Eype and the view of Bridport.

Down House Farm, on the south-eastern slopes, was given to the National Trust [1966] by playwright Robert Cedric Sherriff [1896-1975].

Registered unit CL 48.

SYMONDSBURY

SY 453 909

Four Foot Common

2.52 acres of grassy old quarries in a cliffside depression crossed by footpath number 33, which is the Dorset Coast Path, midway between Eyne Mouth and West Bay.

Registered unit CL 137.

TOLLER PORCORUM

SY 550 963

Barrowland Lane

0.62 acres of roadside verge, with blackthorn scrub and a local authority picnic area.

Registered unit CL 168.

TOLPUDDLE

SY 792 946

Village Green

0.25 acres, including the ageing Martyrs' Tree, a sycamore at which the alleged conspirators met, given to the National Trust by Sir Ernest Debenham to mark the centenary of the "Dorchester Unionists" [1834-1934]. Their contribution to trades union history, having formed the Tolpuddle Friendly Society for which the six were transported to Australia, was commemorated by a large Trades Union Congress gathering.

The green is a leafy triangle of grass on the slope above the River Piddle, facing an attractive range of thatched cottages. The village street is on one side, at the junction with a lane into the meadows, to Affpuddle.

Registered unit VG 66.

TURNERS PUDDLE

SY 837 940

Black Hill Heath

70.85 acres, at the northern boundary of the parish and the extremity of the Dorset heaths in this direction. Nightjars breed in the heather and there is a line of three Bronze Age round barrows.

Bridleway number 5 climbs from Turners Puddle hamlet, over the middle of Black Hill, and Bere Regis bridleway 33 runs along the north-east side. Footpath 3 flanks the north-west side, and footpath 6 strikes off across the southern half. Picturesque and unenclosed with ferny oaks fringing the southern slope.

Registered unit CL 254.

VERWOOD

SU 086 092

Car Park

0.02 acres, at the crossroads in the centre of the old part of the village, which has now mushroomed into a town. Owned by the parish council. One presumes that the registration did not depend upon a communal right to park motor vehicles; it could be argued that parking provision should be for legitimate users of the common, rather than its total sacrifice for the convenience of shoppers.

Registered unit CL 86.

VERWOOD   SU 077 083
Dewlands Common

43.36 acres of gorse heath, with rights registered to collect this as furze faggots, plus the turning out of cows, digging peat turves, and collecting and removing water.

Covered by four adjoining registrations. Lies on the south-west side of what is now virtually a town, crossed by footpath number 82 in the south and footpath 24 to the north.

Registered units CL 50, CL 81, CL 82 and CL 323.

VERWOOD   SU 091 098
Stephen's Castle

1.92 acres, being the northern corner of the pitted gravel-dug hillock beside the Wild Church Bottom plantation of Ringwood Forest. Bridleway number 6 runs along the western side.

The name seems to be an allusion to a Stephen or Stephens of gravel digging fame rather than a memory of some ancient fortress. That said there is a military association in that these and nearby pits provided aggregates for the making of the Phoenix caissons which combined to become Mulberry Harbours when towed across the English Channel to the sands of Normandy [1944].

Registered unit ?CL 77.

VERWOOD   SU 083 057
Three Legged Cross

3.3 acres, being the Recreation Ground, which is owned by the parish council.

Registered unit CL 108.

WAREHAM   SY 905 877
Portland Meadow

35.22 acres, immediately north-west of Wareham Common and divided from it by a water-meadow ditch. On the north side the boundary is the River Piddle. Estover rights include a "foreshare in hay". The meadow's primary purpose was the growing and cutting of lush grass — grazing was therefore restricted to the late summer and winter months, from 1 August to 6 April.

Footpath number 3 runs close to the southern side but does not enter the meadow. There is, however, a right of public access "for air and exercise" under section 193 of the Law of Property Act 1925.

Registered unit CL 136.

WAREHAM   SY 921 873

Town Pound

0.02 acres, at the end of Pound Lane, being situated at the point where the Town Walls drop down to the River Frome in the south-west corner of the old part of the town. Not only would it have been easy to provide water for impounded stock at this location, but strays came here on their own accord, in order to drink, and effectively give themselves up.

Registered unit CL 90.

WAREHAM   SY 920 874

Town Walls

26.57 acres, being the ramparts that Alfred the Great built before the principal Danish invasion [892]. Wareham's walls were part of the defences of the Wessex coastal frontier, the "Burghal Hidage" that held back the tide of European unrest. They were strengthened by Edward the Elder. Eventually, around the year 1000, the earthen bank of the town walls was topped by a curtain of stonework and the ditch was recut in the twelfth century.

Wareham's fortifications form three sides of a square with the River Frome utilised as a natural moat along the southern flank.

The massive, grassy bank of the Town Walls is stranded amongst development and parking areas in the untidy quarter of the town opposite Streche Road. It is here that the earthwork is at its stoutest with the top being 26 feet above the ditch. This section of the old wall is known as the Bloody Bank, remembering the torture and execution of astrologer Peter de Pomfret [23 May 1213] for wrongly predicting the end of King John's harsh reign.

Footpaths run along most of the top and there is also a general right of public access "for air and exercise" under section 193 of the Law of Property Act 1925.

Registered unit CL 22.

WAREHAM   SY 910 874

Wareham Common

79.1 acres of meadow and semi-scrubby gravel hillside stretching for a mile along the valley of the River Piddle, north-west of the town. Reached from below Christmas Close by footpaths numbered 15, 19 and 4, of which the latter then forks north, and footpath 3 continues to its western extremity.

Crossed by the Waterloo–Weymouth railway and also a dyke dated to the Dark Ages and probably contemporary with the Battery Bank at Binnegar, as a final line of defence against a threat that was coming from the north.

There is a right of public access "for air and exercise" under section 193 of the Law of Property Act 1925.

Registered unit CL 23.

WEST PARLEY   SZ 089 988
Ralph's Barrow

0.8 acres, including the relict heathland plot that contains the Bronze Age Ralph's Barrow amid streets of cosy suburbia.

Registered unit CL 174.

WHIT[E]CHURCH CANONICORUM   SY 405 945
Hardown Hill

60.42 acres of heather and gorse-clad chert plateau overlooking the Marshwood Vale and the Morcombelake bowl from 650 feet. Skyline cemetery of seven Bronze Age burial mounds or cairns across the middle of the hill, dating from 2000 BC.

The peaks are South Bullen and High Bullen, and in the west The Toyte — "tout" being a Dorset name for viewpoint coastal hills — with former quarrying for chert rubble being visible at Johnny Vizer's Pits.

The National Trust owns 25 acres, from south to north in the central part of the multi-spurred hill. It is reached and crossed by numerous public paths (numbered 35, 28, 31, 29, 32 and 85) plus byway 89. The access is from just about all sides — Verriott's Lane, Love Lane, Taylor's Lane, Loscombewell's Road, and Ryall Road.

Freedom of public access on foot across the Trust owned sections, which were given to the nation by Mrs Angela Scott-Nicholson [1967].

Registered unit CL 45.

WIMBORNE ST GILES   SU 060 097
Boys Wood

3.55 acres, of dense deciduous woodland, being the north-east corner of a much larger plantation. Footpath number 8 runs along the eastern edge, from the B3081 at the road junction on the bend beside Woodside Cottage.

Registered unit CL 114.

WIMBORNE ST GILES   SU 065 095
Sutton Common

75.2 acres, of enclosed fields beside the road junction opposite Sutton Hill Farm, half a mile west of Verwood.

Registered unit CL 141.

WINFRITH NEWBURGH
Knighton Common
0.8 acres, being the old droveway that is now footpath 5, leading north from the A352 at Knighton Farm to the cluster of thatched cottages that are dwarfed by the Atomic Energy Establishment.
Registered unit CL 98.

WINTERBORNE HOUGHTON
ST 820 046
The Lawn
0.05 acres as a wedge of ground where footpath number 1 strikes off eastwards from the Bulbarrow road out of this high chalkland village. Opposite is footpath 6. On the slope of the hill above the parish church and the thatched quarter of the village street.
Registered unit CL 222.

WINTERBORNE ZELSTON
SY 898 976
Manor Waste
0.72 acres of roadside grass, enhancing the thatched chalkland setting of a cul-de-sac village beside the Winterborne stream. Such waters only flow in winter. Formal manorial waste, with disputed rights, subject to local authority protection.
Registered unit CL 109.

WINTERBOURNE ST MARTIN
SY 646 889
Village Green
0.7 acres of grass, with specimen trees, between the parish church and the main road in the centre of the linear village of Martinstown.
Registered unit VG 32.

WINTERBOURNE ABBAS
SY 618 906
The Green
0.1 acres, beside the A35 and Copyhold Lane, which becomes bridleway number 1. The name has its origins in mediaeval tenure, for land leased at the discretion of the lord of the manor.
Owned by the district council.
Registered unit VG 22.

WOOL
SY 820 875
Burton Common
0.52 acres, being a north-westerly offshoot of Burton Heath.
Registered unit CL 96.

WOOL

SY 823 874

Burton Heath

58.3 acres, now largely covered with sallow scrub and damp woodland, on the south side of the River Frome. Beside the lane from East Burton to Moreton.
Registered unit CL 74.

WORTH MATRAVERS

SY 973 774

Village Pond

0.1 acres including the stone-kerbed pond in a pure Purbeck setting, to a backdrop of stone-roofed cottages. In recent times the water has been black with natterjack toad tadpoles, which is something of a puzzle as these rare amphibians burrow in sand — which is an equal rarity hereabouts.
Owned by the parish council.
Registered unit VG 21.

Corfe Common: the best mediaeval landscape and ruins in Dorset, now in National Trust care, as drawn by Alfred Dawson in 1882.

Bibliography

If you would like to find out more about the subject then the Open Spaces Society is the best place to start.

Commons, greens and Dorset are well covered in this useful short-list. Postage and packing of the books are included in the quoted prices and the addresses for both Open Spaces Society and Dorset Publishing Company are given at the front of the present title.

OSS publications

Our Common Right, Kate Ashbrook, Open Spaces Society, 1987 (free to OSS members, 50p to non-members)

Our Common Land, The Law and History of Commons and Village Greens, Paul Clayden, Open Spaces Society, 1985, reissue 1992 (£6 to OSS members, £9.50 to non-members)

Getting Greens Registered, A Guide to Law and Procedure for Town and Village Greens, Open Spaces Society, 1995 (£6.50 to OSS members, £9 to non-members)

Rights of Way, A Guide to Law and Practice, John Riddall and John Trevelyan, Open Spaces Society and Ramblers' Association, 1992 (£20.50 hardback, £14 paperback)

Making Space, Wendy Lutley, Open Spaces Society, 1992 (£7 to OSS members, £10.50 to non-members)

Other publications

An Outline of the Law relating to Common Land and Public Access to the Countryside, by B. Harris and G. Ryan, Sweet & Maxwell, 1967

The Law of Commons, by G.D. Gadsden, Sweet & Maxwell, 1988

The Common Lands of England and Wales, by W.G. Hoskins and L. Dudley Stamp, Collins New Naturalist series, 1967

Report of the Royal Commission on Common Land, Cmnd 462, 1958

Report of the Common Land Forum, Countryside Commission, 1986

More about Dorset

Dorset National Trust Guide, by Rodney Legg, Dorset Publishing Company, 1992 (£9.95)

Hardy's Wessex Locations, F.P. Pitfield, Dorset Publishing Company, 1992 (£9.95)

Literary Dorset, by Rodney Legg, Dorset Publishing Company, 1990 (£9.95)

National Trust Dorset, by Rodney Legg and Colin Graham, Dorset Publishing Company, 1987 (£18)

Purbeck Island, by Rodney Legg, Dorset Publishing Company, 1989 (£7.95)

Captions — in sequence —
for the first part of the
photographic section

VILLAGE POND: this prehistoric dewpond, dating from 1000 BC, is the reason for the location of Ashmore on top of the chalklands of Cranborne Chase.

MEDIAEVAL PASTURE: ponies grazing on Corfe Common, which is owned by the National Trust, in the heart of the Isle of Purbeck.

RIVERSIDE RAMPARTS: skyline earthworks of Poundbury Camp above meadows beside the River Frome, north-west of Dorchester.

HILL-FORT: Poundbury Camp, dating from the Iron Age, was Dorchester's traditional fairground and gives the best view of the county town.

WATER-MEADOWS: showing the previous riverside view in reverse, from the defences of Poundbury Camp — which is also registered common land.

TOWN GREEN: centrepiece of Dorchester's eastern suburb, at Fordington.

NATIVE HEATH: Dorset's biggest block of common land is Holt Heath, which is owned by the National Trust and managed by English Nature.

MUDDY PATH: into Holt Heath, and not untypical of the wilder side of country walking.

BLACKMORE VALE: open and unenclosed at Lydlinch Common.

Second batch of captions,
onwards from the picture above

EMBATTLED TOWER: of St Nicholas's parish church, beside the village green at Nether Compton.

NATIONAL GRID: crossing National Trust land at Pamphill Green, near Wimborne.

CHESIL BEACH: Portlanders registered common land rights along the great bank of pebbles that links their island with the mainland.

TWO RUINS: mediaeval walls of St Andrew's, the former parish church of Portland, with common land cliffside above Church Ope Cove being dominated by Rufus Castle.

ROCKY SHORE: partly quarried and with derricks for lowering boats into the sea, north-east of Portland Bill.

VILLAGE POUND: for impounding stray stock, on National Trust land at Holt.

THE STOCKS: for punishment by physical restraint, on the village green at Sturminster Marshall.

RESTORED MAYPOLE: at the centre of the Market Place in Sturminster Marshall.

PATH JUNCTION: well signed amid coastal undergrowth at Eype Down, between Thorncombe Beacon and Symondsbury.

MARTYRS' TREE: leaves of the famous sycamore on the village green at Tolpuddle, shrine of trades unionism, with a young replacement planted by the National Trust